POETIC STUDIES.

BY

ELIZABETH STUART PHELPS,

AUTHOR OF "THE GATES AJAR," ETC., ETC.

BOSTON:
JAMES R. OSGOOD AND COMPANY,
LATE TICKNOR & FIELDS, AND FIELDS, OSGOOD, & CO.
1875.

University Press: Welch, Bigelow, & Co.,
Cambridge.

CONTENTS.

THAT NEVER WAS ON SEA OR LAND.

I DREAMED that same old dream again last night;
You know I told you of it once, and more:
The sun had risen, and looked upon the sea,
And turned his head and looked upon the shore,
As if he never saw the world before.

What mystic, mythic season could it be?
It was October with the heart of May.
How count they time within love's calendar?
Dreaming or waking, I can only say
It was the morning of our wedding-day.

I only know I heard your happy step,
As I sat working on my wedding-day
Within my usual place, my usual task ;
You came and took the pen, and laughing,
"Nay!"
You said, "no more this morning! Come away!"

And I, who had been doing dreamily
Within my dream some fitful thing before,
(My pen and I were both too tired to stop,)
Drew breath, — dropped all my work upon the
floor,
And let you lead me mutely to the door,

And out into a place I never saw,
Where little waves came shyly up and curled

Themselves about our feet; and far beyond
As eye could see, a mighty ocean swirled.
"We go," you said, "alone into the world."

But yet we did not go, but sat and talked
Of usual things, and in our usual way;
And now and then I stopped myself to think,—
So hard it is for work-worn souls to play,—
Why, after all it is our wedding-day!

The fisher-folk came passing up and down,
Hither and thither, and the ships sailed by,
And busy women nodded cheerily;
And one from out a little cottage came,
With quiet porches, where the vines hung
high,

And wished us joy, and "When you 're tired," she said,
"I bid you welcome; come and rest with me."
But she was busy like the rest, and left
Us only out of all the world to be
Idle and happy by the idle sea.

And there were colors cast upon the sea
Whose names I know not, and upon the land
The shapes of shadows that I never saw;
And faintly far I felt a strange moon stand, —
Yet still we sat there, hand in clinging hand,

And talked, and talked, and talked, as if it were
Our last long chance to speak, or you to me

Or I to you, for this world or the next;
And still the fisherwomen busily
Passed by, and still the ships sailed to the
sea.

But by and by the sea, the earth, the sky,
Took on a sudden color that I knew;
And a wild wind arose and beat at them.
The fisherwomen turned a deadly hue,
And I, in terror, turned me unto you,

And wrung my wretched hands, and hid my
face.
"O, now I know the reason, Love," I said,
"We 've talked, and talked, and talked the live-
long day,

Like strangers, on the day that we were wed;
For I remember now that you were dead!"

I woke afraid: around the half-lit room
The broken darkness seemed to stir and creep;
I thought a spirit passed before my eyes;
The night had grown a thing too dread for
 sleep,
And human life a lot too sad to weep.

Beneath the moon, across the silent lawn,
The garden paths gleamed white, — a mighty
 cross
Cut through the shadowed flowers solemnly:
Like heavenly love escaped from earthly dross,
Or heavenly peace born out of earthly loss.

And wild my uncalmed heart went questioning it:
"Can that which never has been ever be?"
The solemn symbol told me not, but lay
As dumb before me as Eternity,
As dumb as *you* are when you look at me.

DIVIDED.

If an angel that I know
Should now enter, sliding low
Down the shaft of quiet moonlight that rests upon the floor;
And if she should stir and stand
With a lily in her hand,
And that smile of treasured stillness that she wore,

Should I, falling at her feet,
Brush or kiss her garments sweet?

Would their lowest least white hem upon me
unworthy, fall?
Or would she guarded, stand,
Drop the lily in my hand,
And go whispering as she vanished, "This is
all"?

THE LOST WINTER.

DEEP-HEARTED as an untried joy
  The warm light blushes on the bay,
And placid as long happiness
  The perfect sky of Florida.

Silent and swift the gulls wheel by, —
  Fair silver spots seen flittingly
To sparkle like lost thoughts, and dip
  And vanish in a silver sea.

And green with an immortal spring
  The little lonely islands stand;

And lover-like, the winds caress
  The fresh-plucked roses in my hand.

And sweet with all the scents of June,
  And gentle with the breath of May,
And passionate with harvest calm,
  Dawns the strange face of Christmas-day.

O vanished world of ache and chill!
  If purple-cold the shadows blow
Somewhere upon the shrunken cheeks
  Of wan, tormented drifts of snow;

And if, beneath the steady stare
  Of a pale sunset's freezing eye,

The coming tempest, lurking, stabs
  The lonely traveller hurrying by,—

What art can make me understand?
  What care I, can I care to know?
Star-like, among the tender grass,
  The little white wild-flowers show!

There is no winter in the world!
  There is no winter anywhere!
Earth turns her face upon her arm,
  And sleeps within the golden air.

If once within the story told—
  Of peace or pain, of calm or strife—

The clear revealéd sequences
Of every finished human life,

It chanceth that the record reads:
This wanderer, something torn and tossed
By certain storms he had passed through,
And something faint and chilly, lost

Just here a little while the sense
Of winter from his heavy heart,
And felt within his life the roots
Of spring eternal stir and start;

Could not one blessed little while,
For very happiness, believe

That anywhere upon God's earth
Souls could be cold and worn and live, —

That blessed once a glory were
Enough, I think, to crown one's days.
O swift-departing days of youth,
Lend me your evanescent grace

Of fancy, while my graver years
Like happy children rise and bless
The shadow of the memory of
Love's sweet and helpless selfishness!

Ah, many, many years shall learn
To blush and bloom as young years may,
But only once the soul forget
All else but its own Florida!

APPLE-BLOSSOMS.

Cold Care and I have run a race,
  And I, fleet-foot, have won
A little space, a little hour,
  To find the May alone.

I sit beneath the apple-tree,
  I see nor sky nor sun;
I only know the apple-buds
  Are opening one by one.

You asked me once a little thing,—
  A lecture or a song

To hear with you; and yet I thought
  To find my whole life long

Too short to bear the happiness
  That bounded through the day,
That made the look of apple-blooms,
  And you, and me, and May!

For long between us there had hung
  The mist of love's young doubt;
Sweet, shy, uncertain, all the world
  Of trust and May burst out.

I wore the flowers in my hair,
  Their color on my dress;

Dear Love! whenever apples bloom
  In Heaven, do they bless

Your heart with memories so small,
  So strong, so cruel-glad?
If ever apples bloom in Heaven,
  I wonder are *you* sad?

Heart! yield thee up thy fruitless quest
  Beneath the apple-tree;
Youth comes but once, love only once,
  And May but once to thee!

RAIN.

What can the brown earth do,
Drenched and dripping through
To the heart, and dazzled by the sight
Of the light
That cometh after rain?

What can the hurt life do,
Healing through and through,
Caught and captured by the slow increase
Of the peace
That cometh after pain?

I would not miss the flower
Budded in the shower
That lives to lighten all the wealthy scene
Where rain has been,
That blossoms after pain !

PETRONILLA.

Of Peter's daughter, it is said, men told,
While yet she breathed, a tale as sad as life,
As sweet as death; which, now she sleeps, has
lent
The borrower Time its lighter tints, and holds
Only the shadowed outline of a grief
Before our eyes.
Thus much remains. She lived,
Yet lived not; breathed, yet stifled; ate, but
starved;
The ears of life she had, but heard not; eyes,

But saw not; hands, but handled neither bud
Nor fruit of joy: for the great word of God,
In some dim crevice of eternal thought
Which he called *Petronilla,* had gone forth
Against her — for her — call it what we may,
And, bending to his will unerringly,
As bends the golden feather of the grain
Before the footsteps of the mailed west-wind,
Since childhood she had lain upon her bed
In peace and pain, nor had ever raised her
body
Once to its young lithe length, to view the dawn
Of all her young lithe years, nor had once laid
Her little feverish feet upon the face
Of the cool, mocking, steadfast floor which
laughed

When other girls, with other thinking done
Some time in Heaven about their happy names,—
Set like a song about their happy names,—
Tripped on it like a trill.

As one may see
Upon the hushed lips of a Sabbath-day
A church door sliding softly as a smile,
To let the solemn summer sunshine in
To dream upon, but neither guess nor tell
The dusky week-day secrets which the dome
Whispers the darkened niches and the nave,
Where in the purple silence which they love
The marble angels sleep, or weep, or sing,
(Who knoweth what they do on Monday mornings?)
So slides the tale on Petronilla, left

Upon a certain dull, wan day alone,
Her face turned on her pillow to the room
Wherein the wise and faithful met (for faith
With wisdom married then; none forbid the
banns
Within the temple of the hearts of men),
To break their bread with Peter, and discourse
Of all the sacred, secret things; the hopes,
The fears, the solemn ecstasies, and dreams,
And deeds, which held life in the arms of death,
For the first namers of the name of Christ.
And lying there, at rest, adream, asleep,
She scarce could tell her state, so dim it was,
Such lifeless reflex of the hueless day,
A voice struck Petronilla,— Peter's voice,
Solemn and mighty as a lonely wave

Upon an untrod shore. "O brethren, hark!
Ye know not what ye say; your minds are dark.
O ye of little faith, I show you then!
By his great power I show you. Watch with
me,
For he is here. Abase your heads; he lives;
It is his will I do his will, and show
The power of God in that he once hath lived
And died, but lives to work his glory still, —
To work his wish, unargued, undisturbed,
Without resistance or appeal or blame,
Upon the creature which his hands have made.
Were it his choice to raise yon maiden now
From out the coffin of her bed, and bid
Her step, — or live; it means the same, — what
then?

Is that too much for him to do? What now?
Is that too hard? Increase your faith! Be-
hold!"

Awake, asleep, adream, or all, or none,
What ailèd Petronilla? The world spun
Like a frail spindle in a woman's hands.
And all her breath went from her, and her sight,
At the faint fancy of her father, still,
Alone, alight within the room; as solemn
And sad and glad as had a vision been
Of a choice taper set to spend itself,
And blaze and waste upon an altar's brow,
Not taught nor knowing wherefore, — burning
out,
Since that 's a taper's nature, and enough.

And faint the fancy of his face, if his
It were. And faint the fancy of his voice,
Which lost its way, so Petronilla thought,
Or twice or thrice, before it bridged the bit
Of fanciful, faint sunlight which crawled in
Between his pitying, awful face and hers,
And "Petronilla," sighing softly, said,
And "Petronilla!" ringing cried, "Arise!
"Now, in the name of Christ who lived for thee,
I bid thee live, and rise, and walk!"
                                        Erect,
Unaided, with a step of steel, she rose.
What should she do but rise? And walked; how else?
For God had said it, sent it, dropped it down,
The sweetest, faintest fancy of her life.

And fancying faintly how her feet dropped far
Below the dizzy dancing of her eyes,
Adown the listening floor; and fancying
How all the rising winds crept mutely up
The court, and put their arms around her neck
For joy; and how for joy the sun broke through
The visor which the envious day had held
Across his happy face, and kissed her hair;
And fancying faintly how those men shrank back,
And pulled their great gray beards at sight of
her,
And nodded, as becometh holy men,
Approvingly, at wonders, as indeed
They 'd bade her walk themselves, — so musingly,
As she had been a fancy of herself,

She found herself live, warm and young, within
The borders of the live, warm world.
                                        But still,
As faintly as a fancy fell the voice
Of Peter: "Serve us, daughter, at the board."
And dimly as a fancy served she them,
And sweetly as a fancy to and fro
Across the gold net of the lightening day
She passed and paused.
                        Caught in its meshes fast;
Tangled into the happy afternoon,
Tangled into the sense of life and youth,
Blind with the sense of motion, leap of health,
And wilderness of undiscovered joy,
Stood Petronilla. Down from out her hand
A little platter dropped, and down upon

Her hands her face dropped, broken like the ware
Of earth that sprinkled all the startled floor,
And down upon her knees her face and hands
Fell, clinging to each other; crouching there
At Peter's feet, — her father's feet, — she gave
One little, little longing cry, — no more;
And like the fancy of a cry, — so faint;
And like the angel of a cry, — so brave.
For Peter's face had lifted like the heavens,
Above the presence of the holy men,
Above the maiden serving in the sun,
Above — God help him! — God's own princely
gift,
The pity which a father bears his child.
And far and calm as heaven is shone his smile,
And far and still as heaven is fell his voice,

Yet held a cadence like a prisoned pain,
As one twice-wrecked upon the same bare shore.
"The Lord hath chosen Petronilla. Hearken!
Whom he will choose, he chooseth: some to honor,
Some to dishonor; this to be and bear,
And that to dare and do; these bear his swords,
And these his chains. Nay, but, O man! what then?
Who art thou that shalt mould the mood of God,
Or search his meaning, or defy his will?
On Petronilla he will work his power.
O, what is Petronilla? What am I?
Nay, nay, my child, I tremble; this is wrong.
Thou moanest; that is strange, for he is here

To show his glory on thy young, bent head,
And little smile and hands. O, lift them up
Before him, while I speak the word he sent.
For, by the love of him who died for thee,
Commandment comes ; and I must bid thee turn
And lay thee down upon thy patient bed
Again ; for what am I, and what art thou ?
So turn and lay thee down. Behold it, Lord !
'T is finished, Master ! Petronilla, go.
God's hand is on thee, O my child ; God's grace
Go with thee. Brethren, see ! His will is done,
And shall be done upon us evermore."
And there the wonder fell, so runs the tale ;
For Petronilla turned her dumb as death,
And laid her down upon her empty bed,
Where a long sunbeam warm as life had curled ;

And crept within it, white as sifted snow,
Nor ever raised her slender length again,
Nor ever dropped her foot upon the floor,
Nor ever felt the winds from up the court
Weave arms about her neck; nor ever found
Herself entangled more within the gold
Warp of the moving, merry world; nor once
Again knew even the pallid happiness
Which comes of serving holy men; nor felt
The leap of life within her shrivelled veins.
And there the legend breaks: what good or ill
Struck arms or folded wings about the heart
Of Petronilla; how fared she, prisoned
Behind the bars of that untragic woe,
The bearing of an old familiar fate
From which long use has rubbed the gilding out,

To which the wonted hours have set themselves
So sorely they can neither smile nor sigh
To think of it, but only drop the lids
Across their leaden eyes for wondering
What a glad chance an unworn grief must be;
What solemn musings marshalled in his mind
Who was the Rock on which Christ built a
church
Of such as love nor son nor daughter more
Than him, — we know not; rude our guesses
are,
And rough; and mar the shady, sacred hush
Which the raised fingers of the years enforce.

The story slips, — an echo like the voice
Of far-off, falling water yet unseen;

A puzzle, like our next-door neighbor's life ;
A lesson which an angel on the wing
Might drop, but linger not to read to us,
Or mark the stint. Each heart steals forth alone
A little after twilight, and takes home
The leaf, the line, appointed unto it.

TWO IFS.

If it might only be
That in the singing sea,
The living, lighted sea,
There were a place for you to creep
Away, among the tinted weeds, and sleep, —
A cradled, curtained place for you
To take the happy rest for two!

And then if it might be
Appointed unto me
(God knows how sweet to me!)

To plunge into the sharp surprise
Of burning battle's blood and dust and cries,
    And face the hottest fire for you,
    And fight the bitter fight for two!

A QUESTION.

If there be a land
Where our longings stand,
Like angels strong and sweet
With wings at head and feet,
Released from their long ward
And durance, put on guard
For strength and meetness,
All the stronger for their sweetness,
All the sweeter for their strength, —
In such a land at length,
I wonder, would it ever be
That I could give a little love to thee?

If in such a place
I should see a face
Seen now so long ago
That I should scarcely know
If it might be the same ;
And if one spoke my name,
However faintly,
In the old way, — stealing saintly,
Like a chant upon my ear, —
In such a place I fear
Me, it could never, never be
That thou couldst have a little love from me.

IN TEETH OF FATE.

LET us sit in our darkening weather,
Dear Heart! alone together
For a while,
And talk it all over bravely.
Nay, lift me not up that white, sweet smile;
We 'll face what is coming bravely or gravely, —
But I cannot bear that smile.

No, I did not say the dying,
But those departing, flying
Far away,

Smile so. Come a little nearer!
  I can better think what I had to say.
My darling, my darling! stay nearer, be dearer!
  We will talk some other day.

"DID YOU SPEAK?"

I SAW the prettiest picture
  Through a garden fence to-day,
Where the lilies look like angels
  Just let out to play,
And the roses laugh to see them
  All the sweet June day.

Through a hole behind the woodbine,
  Just large enough to see
(By begging the lilies' pardon)
  Without his seeing me,

My neighbor's boy, and Pharaoh,
  The finest dog you 'll see,

If you search from Maine to Georgia,
  For a dog of kingly air,
And the tolerant, high-bred patience
  The great St. Bernards wear,
And the sense of lofty courtesy
  In breathing common air.

I called the child's name, — "Franko!"
  Hands up to shield my eyes
From the jealous roses, — "Franko!"
  A burst of bright surprise
Transfixed the little fellow
  With wide, bewildered eyes.

"Franko!" Ah, the mystery!
  Up and down, around,
Looks Franko, searching gravely
  Sky and trees and ground,
Wise wrinkles on the eyebrows!
  Studying the sound.

"O Franko!" Puzzled Franko!
  The lilies will not tell;
The roses shake with laughter,
  But keep the secret well;
The woodbine nods importantly.
  "Who spoke?" cried Franko. "Tell!"

The trees do not speak English;
  The calm great sky is dumb;

The yard and street are silent;
  The old board-fence is mum;
Pharaoh lifts his head, but, ah!
  Pharaoh too is dumb.

Grave wrinkles on his eyebrows,
  Hand upon his knee,
Head bared for close reflection,
  Lighted curls blown free, —
The child's soul to the brute's soul
  Goes out earnestly.

From the child's eyes to the brute's eyes,
  And earnestly and slow,
The child's young voice falls on my ear
  "Did you speak, Pharaoh?"

The bright thought growing on him, —
  "Did *you* speak, Pharaoh?"

. . . . .

I can but think if Franko
  Would teach us all his way
Of listening and trusting, —
  The wise, wise Franko way! —
The world would learn some summer
  To hear what dumb things say.

BROKEN RHYTHM.

My oars keep time to half a rhyme,
  That slips and slides away from me.
Across my mind, like idle wind,
  A lost thought beateth lazily.

Adream, afloat, my little boat
  And I alone steal out to sea.
One vanished year, O Lost and Dear!
  You rowed the little boat for me.

Ah, who can sing of anything
  With none to listen lovingly?
Or who can time the oars to rhyme
  When left to row alone to sea?

ON THE BRIDGE OF SIGHS.

It chanceth once to every soul,
Within a narrow hour of doubt and dole,

Upon Life's Bridge of Sighs to stand,
"A palace and a prison on each hand."

O palace of the rose-heart's hue!
How like a flower the warm light falls from you!

O prison with the hollow eyes!
Beneath your stony stare no flowers arise.

O palace of the rose-sweet sin!
How safe the heart that does not enter in!

O blessed prison-walls! how true
The freedom of the soul that chooseth you!

HIDE-AND-GO-SEEK.

HAPPINESS has found me out,
Found me out at last!
O, she 's dogged me round about;
All my hurrying life she 's chased me,
Treading hard and hot she 's raced me,
Almost touched me, all but faced me, —
Here she is, at last!

Wary were you, Happiness!
Patient to the last!
From your thankless business

Laggard Time has come to free you.
Always driven by Fate to flee you,
Never did I think to see you
    Track me down at last!

GIVING OF THANKS.

DEEP in the brooding shadow of thy wing,
 Hidden and hushed and harbored here,
My soul for very stillness cannot sing;
 A word would rend the silence, and a tear
Of joy affront the sense of cool and dark and rest.

Unto the music of thine endless calm
 Sing thou then for me! Thy glad child
Sheltered and saved, wrapped all about from
 harm,
 Happy to be helpless, — and thy child;
Can only turn and sleep within the blessed rest,

Can only drop the gifts which thou hast given
 Back in thy lavish hand. O wealth
Of fulness! that for life, for love, for Heaven,
 For *thyself*, thou shouldst thank thyself
In me; and leave me mute and motionless, —
 at rest.

FEELING THE WAY.

Feeling the way, — and all the way up hill;
But on the open summit, calm and still,
The feet of Christ are planted; and they stand
    In view of all the quiet land.

Feeling the way, — and though the way is dark,
The eyelids of the morning yet shall mark
Against the East the shining of his face,
    At peace upon the lighted place.

Feeling the way, — and if the way is cold,
What matter? — since upon the fields of gold
His breath is melting; and the warm winds sing
    While rocking summer days for him.

LEARNING TO PRAY.

My inmost soul, O Lord, to thee
  Leans like a growing flower
Unto the light. I do not know
  The day nor blessed hour
When that deep-rooted, daring growth
  We call the heart's desire
Shall burst and blossom to a prayer
  Within the sacred fire
Of thy great patience; grow so pure,
  So still, so sweet a thing
As perfect prayer must surely be.
  And yet my heart will sing

Because thou seem'st sometimes so near.
  Close-present God! to me,
It seems I could not have a wish
  That was not shared by thee;
It seems I cannot be afraid
  To speak my longings out,
So tenderly thy gathering love
  Enfolds me round about;
It seems as if my heart would break,
  If, living on the light
I should not lift to thee at last
  A bud of flawless white.
And yet, O helpless heart! how sweet
  To grow, and bud, and say:
The flower, however marred or wan,
  Shall not be cast away.

WHAT THE SHORE SAYS TO THE SEA.

EBB–TIDE.

OLD, old,
Centuries old,
How old a love is, who can say?
It is an ancient day
Since thou and I wert wed.
The orbéd sky bent down,
A fiery, scornful crown,
Not craven pale as now,
Live-red to bind thy brow,
Crested red and lonely
Only
To coronet thy head.

Thou, I,
Beneath His eye,
Existed solitary, grand.
O only life! the life of sea and land!
All puny heritage
Of puny love and loss.
Came mimic after us;
Our mighty wedlock meant
More than their supplement.
Ere these, we perfect were,
And are,
In pain and privilege.

My own true-hearted!
Since first He parted
Thee from me,

Behold and see
How dreary, mute,
Bound hand and foot,
Stretched, starved, I lie!
I hear thee stepping by,
And weep to see
Thee yearn to me.
Bound by an awful Will
Forever and forever thou dost move
An awful errand on.
O Love!
Steal up and say, — is there below, above;
In height or depth, or choice or unison,
Of woes a woe like mine, —
To lie so near to thine,
And yet forever and forever to lie still!

WHAT THE SEA SAYS TO THE SHORE.

FLOOD-TIDE.

O Sweet!
I kiss thy feet.
It is permitted me
So much to keep of thee,
So much to give to thee.
Reverently
I touch thy dusky garments' hem.
Thy dazzling feet lie bare;
But now the moonlit air,
In hurrying by, did gaze at them.

Who can guess
The temper of a love denied?
See! to my lips I press,—
I press and hide
Thy sweet
Sad feet,
And cover them from sight of all the world.

Till thou and I were riven apart,
Never was it known
By any one
That storms could tear an ocean's heart.
Nor shall it be again
That storms can cause an ocean pain.
But when He said:
"No farther, thus far, shalt thou go;

And here,
In fear,
Shall thy proud waves be stayed," —
Raging, rebel, and afraid,
What could shore or ocean do?

Fling down thy long loose hair
For a little share
Of the little kiss I still may bring to thee.
O Love! turn unto me!
The hours are short that I may be
Rich though so scantily,
Blest although so broken-hearted.
Sweet my Love! when we are parted,
When unheard orders bid me go
Obedient to an unknown Will,

The pain of pains selects me so,
That I *must* go, and thou lie still.
While yet my lips may hunger near thy feet,
Turn to me, Sweet!

ATALANTA.

Atalanta and I know better!
Distrust you the fable of old,
Of the envious Goddess who set her
On to defeat by tempting her soul
    With the wily bright roll
Of an apple of treacherous gold.

Distrust the story which tells you
She loitered with willing, shy feet.
A doubt on the myth which compels you
Ever to dream that she lingered to lose

In the race, or to choose
In Love's contest an easy defeat!

She never could linger, no, never!
To *help* poor Hippomenes by!
Fleet-footed, stern-hearted, forever,
She keeps to the goal. Let him win if he can!
If he be not the man
Born for winning, why then let him die!

The fable was twisted! I plant a
Firm foot of assurance on this.
Some woman — but not Atalanta —
Lingered to lose; and stooped to enhance
By a sweet trick the chance
Of being defeated by bliss!

A LETTER.

Two things love can do,
    Only two:
Can distrust, or can believe;
It can die, or it can live,
There is no syncope
Possible to love or me.
    Go your ways!

Two things you can do,
    Only two:
Be the thing you used to be,
Or be nothing more to me.

I can but joy or grieve,
Can no more than die or live.
Go your ways!

So far I wrote, my darling, drearily,
But now my sad pen falls down wearily
From out my trembling hand.

I did not, do not, cannot mean it, Dear!
Come life or death, joy, grief, or hope, or fear,
I bless you where I stand!

I bless you where I stand, excusing you,
No speech nor language for accusing you
My laggard lips can learn.

To you — be what you are, or can, to me, —
To you or blessedly or fatefully
　　My heart must turn!

AN AUTUMN VIOLET.

I SAW a miracle to-day!
Where the September sunshine lay
Languidly as a lost desire
Upon a sumach's fading fire,
Where calm some pallid asters trod,
Indifferent, past a golden-rod,
Beside a gray-haired thistle set, —
  A perfect purple violet.

I wonder what it were to miss
The life of spring, and live like this?

To bloom so lone, to bloom so late,
And were it worth the while to wait
So long for such a little day?
And were it not a better way
Never, indeed, (worse might befall,)
To be a violet at all?

So lonely when the spring was gone,
So calm when autumn splendors shone,
So peaceful midst the blazing flowers,
So blessed through the golden hours,
So might have bloomed my love for thee.
It is not, and it cannot be, —
It cannot, must not be, — and yet,
I picked for thee the violet.

DESERTED NESTS.

I 'D rather see an empty bough,—
A dreary, weary bough that hung
As boughs will hang within whose arms
No mated birds had ever sung;

Far rather than to see or touch
The sadness of an empty nest
Where joy has been but is not now,
Where love has been but is not blest.

There is no sadness in the world,
No other like it here or there,—
The sadness of deserted homes
In nests, or hearts, or anywhere.

THE DIFFERENCE.

THE breakers warned them from the sea,
  The late light lured them up the shore;
The jewels of the golden-rod
  Blazed deep as topaz to the core;
The far fields watched them silently
And blessed them like the peace of God.

"If we could always walk," she said,
  "As now we 're walking up the shore,
I think how happy we might be!
  To walk and talk forevermore,

Without a care without a dread,
That were enough for you and me!"

"O cruel-calm! you know," said he,
"The man who dares to spend with you
An hour like this on sea or shore,
Can never teach his fancy to
Practise such sweet humility,
Must all his life go wanting more!"

CONGRATULATION.

You told the story of your love;
  I heard as one who did not hear;
Across the opening lips of hope
  Crept the slow finger of a fear.

Against the kind deceit which hides
  From love's beginning all love's end,
In thoughtful mood I boldly lift
  The honest trouble of a friend.

You 've chosen thus: not thus, indeed,
  I would have chosen fate for you,

And if you missed the possible
 And for the sweet had lost the true ;

If 'neath the perfect palm of love
 You might have knelt, — in kneeling, blest, —
And if you chose instead to wear
 A little rose upon your breast ;

If, for the tidal wave of life
 Mistook a little ripple blue,
While fathoms deep below your line
 The sea's lost treasures sleep for you ;

Why, then, what then? You 've only missed
 A wealth your calm eyes never saw.

Be fate and nature kind to you,
 Yourself unto yourself your law!

No Moses ever part for you
 The wonders of the deep's rich gloom!
Nor ever lead, the dry sands o'er,
 Into the long-lost palm-land's bloom!

Ah! never, never may you know,
 For little waves trip merrily;
And never, never may you know,
 For sweet the little roses be.

And should my doubts and dreams be both
 Blindfold, as dreams and doubts may be;

Should love's unwisdom truer prove
  To you than my wise fears to me;

Since God's own purpose over ours
  Is folded softly like a wing,
And love's best knowledge to love's self
  Must own, I know not anything!

Why then — ah! then. Go you his ways,
  Not mine. His is the summer sea,
On which the little waves shall trip;
  And his the little roses be.

But if into one lot there came
  (As into one I haply knew)

The flower's scent, the forest's strength,
  The depth's reserve, the ripple's hue;

If it fell out to Heaven's mind
  To give one both the sweet and true, —
Though Heaven asked it back again, —
  That lost lot I 'd not change with you.

GOOD-BY.

God be with you! through my losing
  And my grieving, shall I say?
Through my smiling and my hoping,
  God be with you, friend, to-day!

Somewhere, on a Shore of Silver,
  (God be with you on the way!)
In a sunlight sifted richly
  From a thousand skies of May,

In a dream of June's white roses,
  In a chant of waters low,

In a glory of red maples,
  A hush of moonlight upon snow,

In the meanings of the sunrise,
  In the heart of summer rain,
In the soul of purple hazes,
  We will not say good by again.

But the tears dash through my dreaming,
  And the thing I fain would say
Falters into this, — this only:
  God be with you till that day!

TWO FACES.

"WOULD I could see!" I heard one say but now,
"The strongest woman and the tenderest man
That ever God had dared put in the world!"
And I, who did not speak, because one can
Tell out one's sweetest secret to the sky
Sometimes with greater ease than one can speak
It at some others to a friend's close ear,
Went up into the gallery of my soul
Silent and smiling and assured, to see
Some pictures that are hung there on the wall,
Whereat my soul and I on leisure days
Sit gazing and sit thirsting by ourselves.

And one there is that looketh down to me
Less like a face than like a star, for when
With closed eyes I would think what it is like
I only can remember that it shines.
But when I turn again to con and learn
Its lineaments like a lesson in my thought,
The forehead has the look that marble has
When it has drawn the sunlight to its heart.
And if St. John had fought the Dragon, then
He might have had perhaps such eyes as that
(But still I do not tell you what the eyes
Are like, nor can I, and I am not sure,
Indeed, that I should tell you if I could).
O, straight they look the world into the face!
And never have they dropped before its gaze,
And never sunk they down abashed, to hide

A glance of which their own light was ashamed.
And if an unclean thing had chanced to step
Into the presence of such eyes, pierced, scorched,
It would have shrunk before their stabs, but ere
It could have risen to flee, it would have dropped,
And cowered moaning in the dust, because
It felt itself a thing they pitied so!
And then the mouth! — I never saw a mouth,
Another one, that seemed to think and feel
At once like this. If haply lips like these
Had found a word for which the whole round
earth
Were waiting, while they spoke the word, I think
They 'd quiver most because upon that day
The woman that they loved had touched them,
— said,

"Go speak, my lips, and make me proud!" — the most
For that than for the worth of either work or world.

And one there is (across the gallery's width
This picture hangs), a graver face, and touched
A little with a sadness such as that
Which might have fallen on the countenance
Of Esther in the story, when she left
Her throne to perish for her people's sake;
The sadness of a soul bound fast to bear —
Whether by fate or choice it knoweth not —
Within itself the sorrows of a race,
A kind, to which it has no gladder tie
Than the blind old mystery of kin; urged on
By something in its nature like a cry

That will be heard, come life, come death! to lay
Aside the crown, the robe of royalty,
And mediate, a suppliant, for its own.
If she perish, she must perish! — but must go.
Though she perish, let her perish! — let her go.
Soft falls the hair about this other face,
Leaving a shadow like a shadow thrown
By leafless trees upon a snow-drift's brow,
A slender shelter for the dazzling white.
And out from it look steady eyes that hide
Their perfect meaning from the casual gaze,
And out from it there leans a flying smile,
As one smiles turning slowly from the page
In which his heart is left to hear
The sweetest interruption in the world
More languidly than lovingly. I think

You 'd never pause to speculate or guess
Which interruption were the dearer fret
To her, but only what the lesson was
O'er which she bent, and only wonder on
If Esther had a smile like that ; and if
Her people, when they saw it, understood
The half of it ; and if the King will hold,
As did Ahasuerus in the time
Of old, his sceptre out, and ever call
This unqueened Queen in triumph to her throne.

And if there were on earth a tenderer strength ?
Or if there were a stronger tenderness ?
What matters it to me ? for now behold !
That gallery in my longing soul is full,
And God himself came up and shut the door.

LAND-BOUND.

ALL the day the light lies dreaming, dreaming,
    Quietly on the lea.
All the day the ships go sailing, sailing,
    Over an unseen sea.

Sentient, strong, the hill lies couching, crawling,
    Pressed close against the sky,
Pierced by lances quivering, sharp, unerring,—
    The thin masts drifting by.

All the night the breakers, distant, daring,
    Sing straight a solemn song;

Day and night from unguessed ocean greatness
Great winds are borne along.

Night and day my eyes are gazing, straining,
Filled full of land-bound tears.
My land-bound heart is full of little sorrows
And full of little fears.

. . . . .

O happy souls! that soft go sailing, sailing,
Over an unknown sea,
Send some signal of your wafting, wandering,
Across the hills to me!

Across the cruel hills, that stern and steadfast
Sever you and me,
Tell me sometimes of your peaceful, blessed
Life upon the sea!

A MESSAGE.

WAS there ever message sweeter
  Than that one from Malvern Hill,
From a grim old fellow — you remember?
  Dying in the dark at Malvern Hill.
With his rough face turned a little,
  On a heap of scarlet sand,
They found him, just within the thicket,
  With a picture in his hand, —

With a stained and crumpled picture
  Of a woman's aged face;
Yet there seemed to leap a wild entreaty,
  Young and living — tender — from the face

When they flashed the lantern on it,
  Gilding all the purple shade,
And stooped to raise him softly, —
  "That 's my mother, sir," he said.

"Tell her" — but he wandered, slipping
  Into tangled words and cries, —
Something about Mac and Hooker,
  Something dropping through the cries
About the kitten by the fire,
  And mother's cranberry-pies; and there
The words fell, and an utter
  Silence brooded in the air.

Just as he was drifting from them,
  Out into the dark, alone,

(Poor old mother, waiting for your message,
  Waiting with the kitten, all alone !)
Through the hush his voice broke, — " Tell her —
  Thank you, Doctor — when you can,
Tell her that I kissed her picture,
  And wished I 'd been a better man."

Ah, I wonder if the red feet
  Of departed battle-hours
May not leave for us their searching
  Message from those distant hours.
Sisters, daughters, mothers, think you,
  Would your heroes now or then,
Dying, kiss *your* pictured faces,
  Wishing they 'd been better men ?

ESCAPED.

Just before you came,
There stole into the air
A thought without a name.

Such a pretty thought!
Shy, and faint, and fair, —
I wish I could have caught

It when it came,
And brought it unto you;
You would have found its name!

But when I turned, and would
Have gathered it for you,
And clasped it where it stood,

It shook me out a pair
Of unseen little wings,
And vanished in the air.

Do you like to hear
Such foolish little things?
Ah, truly, — tell me, dear!

SONG.

COLDLY the night-wind shivers on the hill-top,
Cold crawls the pale-faced fog from off the sea;
Tossed by the one, and blinded by the other,
Turn I my late steps longing unto thee!

Warm as thy glad hand, held in silence towards
me,
Shines out thy window's light across the lea;
Warm as a flower waiting for the south-wind,
So waits thy sweet face sheltered there for me.

Wild as the gale, and like the mist pervading
The soul of the dark night, and the soul of me,
Hoping or hopeless, for living or for dying,
Turn I my late love forever unto thee!

"OF A FAMILY OF REFORMERS."

PUSH the bursting buds away,
  Throw aside the ripened roses,
Hush the low-voiced waters' play,
  Where the weary sun reposes
      With his head upon his hand,
      Grave and grand!
      Now I stand,
And shade my eyes to see
What life shall mean to me.

Cut the silver-hearted mist
  Stealing softly down the valley;

Blot me out the purple, kissed
  By phantoms crowned in gold, that rally
      Merrily upon the land,
      Gay and grand.
      Here I stand,
And turn my eyes to see
What life may mean to me.

There seems — a path across a hill,
  But little worn (but little lonely),
A climb into the twilight still;
  There seems — a midnight watch, and only
    Through the dark a low command
    (Grave and grand),
    "Still you stand,
And strain your eyes to see
What life to you shall be."

The binding up of bruisèd reeds
  Of thought and act; the steady bearing
Out of scorned purposes to deeds,
  The rest of strife; the doubt of daring, —
    The hope that He will understand
    Why my hand
    (Though I stand)
Trembles at my eyes to see
What else life means to me.

The dropping of love's golden fruit,
  The slowly builded walls of distance,
The outstretched hand, the meeting foot,
  Withdrawn in doubt, and drear, late chance
    Of cooling autumn; wind and sand
    On the land. —
    But I stand,

And brush my tears to see
All that life means to me.

The honest choice of good or ill,
A heart of marble, prayer, and fire,
The strength to do, the power to will
From earth's reluctance, Heaven's desire,
And God's step upon the land
(Grave and grand).
Glad I stand
And lift my eyes to see
The life He sends to me.

A DEAD LILY.

O PLACID, fainted lily !
  You neither toiled nor spun ;
You neither thought nor wrought, or well or
    illy, —
  And now your day is done.

You lived — to be a lily.
  And should I gain or miss
My life's long purposes or well or illy,
  What could I, more than this ?

BENEDICTION.

I WONDER will you take it, Dear,—
My blessing, from me, when you hear
  For what it is you ask me?

The shrouded and averted thing,
With hidden face upon its wing,
  With whose dark name you task me.

The solemn, awful, smiling thing,
With shining face upon its wing,
  And shining hand to hold you.

The promise of a princely friend,
The richest gift I have to send,
  With which my love could fold you.

So light to think! so hard to say!
A bitter thing to give away!
  So sweet an one to borrow!

Yet still, indeed, my dreaming fond
Can never rise nor reach beyond
  The blessing, Dear, — of Sorrow.

"ONLY A CHROMO."

A BLESSING on the Art that dares
(Cold critic, call it what you may!)
Bring precious things to common homes;
A blessing fall on it, I say!

Like Heaven's happy rain, that loves
Upon the just and unjust to fall;
Th' impartial shelter of the skies,
Or sun's heart beating warm for all;

So be it Art's high privilege
To hold a language and a speech

With humble needs; to lay its gifts —
And gladly — in the common reach.

So be it Art's insignia
Of undisputed royalty,
That out of largeness groweth love,
And out of choiceness, charity.

There is my picture, caught and throned
Within four walls for me at last;
My eyes, which never thought to see
Fit semblance of her, hold her fast.

Murillo's Mary! that one face
We call the Immaculate. Ah, see

How goddess-like she fills the room,
How woman-like she leans to me.

I would not garner in my home,
I could not gather to my heart,
A dim gray mockery of that face
Chilled under the engraver's art.

These human colors deepen, glow;
This human flesh will palpitate;
These human eyes, — like human eyes
Alight, alive, — stir, watch, and wait.

Perhaps you wonder why I chose
This single-windowed little room

Where only at the evenfall,
A moment's space, the sunlight's bloom

Shall open out upon the face
I prize so dear; I think, indeed,
There 's something of a whim in that,
And something of a certain need

I could not make you understand,
That solitude or sickness gives
To take in somewhat solemn guise
The blessings that enrich our lives.

I like to watch the late, soft light,—
No spirit could more softly come,—

The picture is the only thing
It touches in the darkening room.

I wonder if to her indeed,
The maiden of the spotless name,
In holier guise or tenderer touch
The annunciating angel came.

Madonna Mary! Here she lives!
See how my sun has wrapped her in!
O solemn sun! O maiden face!
O joy that never knoweth sin!

How shall I name thee? How express
The thoughts that unto thee belong?

Sometimes a sigh interprets them,
At other times, perhaps, a song.

More often still it chanceth me
They grow and group into a prayer
That guards me down my sleepless hours,
A sentry on the midnight air.

But when the morning's monotone
Begins of sickness or of pain,
They catch the key, and, striking it,
They turn into a song again.

Great Master, whose enraptured eyes
Saw maiden Mary's holy face,

Whose human hand could lift and move
An earthly passion from its place,

And set therein the spotless shape
Which Heavenly love itself might wear,
And set thereon the dazzling look
Which Heavenly purity must bear;

Thy blessing on the Art must fall
(If thou couldst speak as thou canst see)
Which brings thy best to common homes,
Thy mighty picture unto me.

A WOMAN'S MOOD.

BECAUSE you cannot pluck the flower,
  You pass the sweet scent by;
Because you cannot have the stars
  You will not see the sky

No matter what the fable means
  Put into English speech;
No matter what the thing may be
  You long for, out of reach.

'T is out of reach, and that 's enough
  For you and me for aye,

And understood in that still speech
  That souls interpret by.

The "little language" of a look,
  A tone, a turn, a touch,
An eloquence that while it speaketh
  Nothing, yet sayeth much.

Suppose that in some steadfast hour
  I offered you the hand
Of a woman's faithful friendliness —
  Ah, hush! I understand.

I spare you speech, to spare you pain;
  Perhaps I 'd spare you more

Than men are made to comprehend,
  If, as I said before,

I held to you that open hand,
  And you should turn away
I hardly know which one of us
  Were hurt the worse that day.

I hardly know the reason why,
  But women are so made;
I could not give a man a rose
  To see it 'neath his tread.

Although he trod on it, indeed,
  To save his very soul

From stifling in the thoughts of me
  Its sweetness might enroll.

I 'd rather he should gather it
  Within his trembling hand
As sacredly as twilight takes
  The shapes of sea and land,

And solemnly as twilight learns,
  In lonely, purple state,
Upon the hills the sun has fled
  To bide its time, and wait.

For what? — to wait for what, you ask?
  I cannot tell, indeed,

For what. I do not know for what.
It is the woman's creed!

I only know I 'd wait, and keep
Steel-loyal and steel-true
Unto the highest hope I held,
Though 't were the saddest, too.

Unto the deepest faith I had
In a created thing;
Unto the largest love I knew,
Though love's delight took wing

And fled away from me, and left
Love's dear regret alone.

The chrism of loving all I could,
  And loving only one.

I think the woman I preferred —
  If I were such a man —
Might lean out helpfully across
  My life's imperfect plan;

Might lend me mercy, grace, and peace
  In fashion womanly,
Although I knew her rarest smile
  Would never shine on me;

I think I 'd say right manfully, —
  And so it all would end, —

Than any other woman's love,
  I 'd rather be *her* friend!

And take the hand she dared not hold,
  Before its courage slips,
And take the word she could not speak
  From off her grieving lips,

And be to her heart what I could
  (We will not mark the line),
And, like a comrade, call her soul
  To walk in peace with mine.

A nobler man for that grave peace,
  I think, dear friend, I were,

And richer were I than to lose
  My love in losing her.

And if I speak a riddle, sir,
  That on your fancy jars, —
You know we 're talking about flowers,
  And thinking about stars!

A MAN'S REPLY.

THAT heart were something cold, I think,
That on the light of stars relied
For daily fire; and cruel is
The perfumed breath of flowers denied
The longing, lifted human hand;
And bitter to the soul, I stand
And fling your woman's fancies back
Beneath the woman's tender feet!
A woman only knoweth love
To know that it is passing sweet,

To know that all her heart is glad,
Or else to know that she is sad
Because it failed her ; and forsooth,
I think she has an extra sense
To love by, granted not to man:
Love's measureless own recompense
Consists in loving : there 's her creed.
A pretty thought, in faith or deed!
A feminine fair thought, but false
To man forever! false as light
To the born blind, as painted fruit
To starving lips ; or as a bright
Departing sail to drowning eyes.
Arch not to me, in mild surprise,
Those glorious calm brows of yours!
Man loveth in another way!

He cannot take the less without
The more; he has a bitter way
In loving, that you know not of;
No tireless, tender, calm resolve
To take Fate's meagre crumbs when dry
From life's feast-tables overswept
And salt them with his hidden, hot,
Vain tears! Contented to be kept
As cup-bearer beside a goddess' place!
Contented so he see her face,
Her dear, denied, sweet face, and die!
O lost, my love! I tell you nay,
You do not, cannot understand;
Man loveth in another way!
He is too strong, or is too weak:
I cannot be the friend you seek!

And yet, in the incertitudes
Of some uncomforted, cold moods,

I cast my soul before you, Sweet!
My very soul beneath your feet,

And, daring and despairing, think
That could I stoop but once and drink,—

One little moment lean above
The sealed, lost fountain of your love,—

Could taste, just taste before I die,
Its sacred, sheltered mystery,—

Could call you for one hour mine!
One little, little hour mine!—

I think I could arise and go
From out your presence then, and know

Myself that possible poised man
Who, living, loving, longing, can

Yet make himself the thing he may, —
Live in the woman's nobler way, —

Love, asking Love no other gauge
Than the exceeding privilege

Of adding by some patient stress.
Of pain, unto the happiness, —

Or be it bright, or be it dim —
Of the sweet soul denied to him.

EVENING PRAYER.

TAKE unto Thyself, O Father!
  This folded day of thine,
  This weary day of mine.
Its ragged corners cut me yet.
O, still the jar and fret!
Father! do not forget
    That I am tired
  With this day of thine.

Breathe thy pure breath, watching Father!
  On this marred day of thine,
  This erring day of mine.

Wash it white of stain and spot,
O, cleanse its every blot!
Reproachful Eyes! remember not
    That I have grieved thee
  On this day of thine!

SATURDAY NIGHT IN THE HARBOR.

THE boats bound in across the bar,
Seen in fair colors from afar,
Grown to dun colors strong and near;
Their very shadows seem to fear
The shadows of a week of harms,
The memories of a week's alarms,
And quiver like a happy sigh
As ship and shadow, drifting by,
Glide o'er the harbor's peaceful face,
Each to its Sabbath resting-place.

And some like weary children come,
With sobbing sails, half sick for home;

And some, like lovers' thoughts, to meet
The veilèd shore, spring daring, sweet;
And some reluctant, in the shade,
The great reef dropt, like souls afraid,
Creep sadly in. Against the shore
Ship unto shadow turneth more
And more. Ships, ocean, shadow, shore!
Part not, nor stir forevermore!

My thoughts sail inward silently,
My week-day thoughts, O God, to thee!
Cold fears, evasive like a star,
And hopes whose gayest colors are
Akin to shades of fear. Wild dreams
Whose unimprisoned sweetness seems
To-night a presence like a blame,

A solid presence like a shame:
And faint temptations with held breath
Make room for cares as dark as death,
Give place to broken aims, that sail
Dismasted from some heart-spent gale.

And those come leaping lightly in,
And these crawl laggard, as a sin
Turned shoreward — Godward — ever must.
My soul sits humble in the dust,
Content to think that in His grace
Each care shall find its Sabbath place,
Content to know that, less or more
No sin can harbor near the shore.

THE LOST POEM.

FLUSHED with fancies, I bethought me,
"Into music I will set them,
Like a pearl into its setting
Of the finest golden fretting;
Never shall the world forget them;
It shall sing me, ring me back the melody;
It shall rise and bless the poem while it bless-
eth me."

But, ah me! some faintness ailed me,
Or it ailed the music rather.

Was it all a stir of gladness?
Was it half a pang of sadness?
Do my best, I could not gather
From my heart's store any chord of harmony;
No other thought was music to me but the
thought of *thee.*

Proud as joy my failure makes me!
Proud I sit and sing about it;
Not in finest poet-fashion,
Not for deepest poet's passion,
Would my soul have gone without it,
While the old earth asketh song or psalmody,
Heart, remember! love shall still the truest
music be!

ALL THE RIVERS.

"All the rivers run into the sea."
Like the pulsing of a river,
The motion of a song,
Wind the olden words along
The tortuous turnings of my thoughts whenever
I sit beside the sea.

"All the rivers run into the sea."
O you little leaping river,

Laugh on beneath your breath!
With a heart as deep as death,
Strong stream, go patient, grave, and hasting
never, —
I sit beside the sea.

"All the rivers run into the sea."
Why the passion of a river?
The striving of a soul?
Calm the eternal waters roll
Upon the eternal shore. At last, whatever
Seeks it — finds the sea.

"All the rivers run into the sea."
O thou bounding, burning river,

Hurrying heart! I seem
To know (so one knows in a dream)
That in the waiting heart of God forever,
Thou too shalt find the sea.

THE END.

Cambridge: Electrotyped and Printed by Welch, Bigelow, & Co.

www.ingramcontent.com/pod-product-compliance
Lightning Source LLC
LaVergne TN
LVHW021413110826
845150LV00007B/1912

9781425510107